NNAT® TEST PREP

- **Grade 3 and 4 Level D**
- **Two Full-Length Practice Tests**
- **96 Full-Color Practice Questions**
- **Answer Key**
- **Sample Questions for Each Test Area**
- **Additional Bonus Questions Online**

Nicole Howard

Thank you for selecting this book.

We'd love to get your feedback on the website where you purchased this book.

By leaving a review, you give us the opportunity to improve our work.

Nicole Howard and the SkilledChildren.com Team

www.skilledchildren.com

Co-authors: Albert Floyd and Steven Beck

First edition.

TABLE OF CONTENTS

INTRODUCTION

The Naglieri Nonverbal Ability Test® (or NNAT®) assesses nonverbal reasoning and general problem-solving abilities and it is often used to determine eligibility for gifted schools and programs.

The NNAT® Test, Level D, is administered for both 3rd a 4th-grade students and it is composed of non-verbal questions; this means that it involves very little reading, writing, or speaking ability. Tests are mainly based on pictures, shapes, and patterns.

The NNAT® Test includes four kinds of questions: Pattern Completion, Reasoning by Analogy, Serial Reasoning, and Spatial Visualization. Level D includes all four-question types.

The Overall Format of the Level D Test

The actual version of the NNAT® Test, Level D, is divided into 48 multiple-choice questions:

- **Pattern Completion** has 10 questions.
- **Reasoning by Analogy** has 14 questions.
- **Serial Reasoning** has 10 questions.
- **Spatial Visualization** has 14 questions.

Students have 30 minutes to complete the test.

How to Use the Content of this Book

Since the NNAT® is an important test in all students' schooling careers; the correct amount of preparation must be performed.

This book will help you prepare your students before test day and will expose them to the format of the test so they'll know what to expect.

This book includes:

- Two full-length NNAT® Level D practice questionnaires.
- Question examples for teachers/parents to help their students approach all of the questions on the test with confidence and determination.
- Answer key with clear explanations.

PRACTICE TEST 1 PATTERN COMPLETION

Pattern Completion

The Pattern Completion session of the NNAT is designed to evaluate the student's skill to visually discern a pattern in the context of a larger picture.

The student's assignment is to identify the hidden area of the image and to select the answer that completes the picture.

EXAMPLE

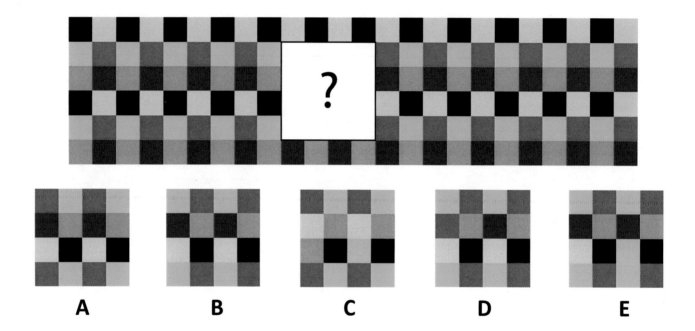

- To answer correctly, carefully observe the boundaries of the missing area.

- The missing square is divided into 16 small squares arranged in 4 rows and 4 columns.

- The square in the upper left corner must be pink. We can exclude answers B, D, E.

- The top right square must be blue. So let's focus on answers A and C.

- The first square on the left in the second row must be black. So the correct answer is A.

1.

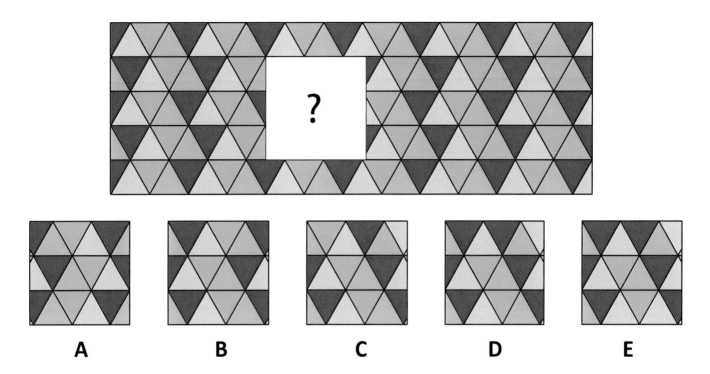

2.

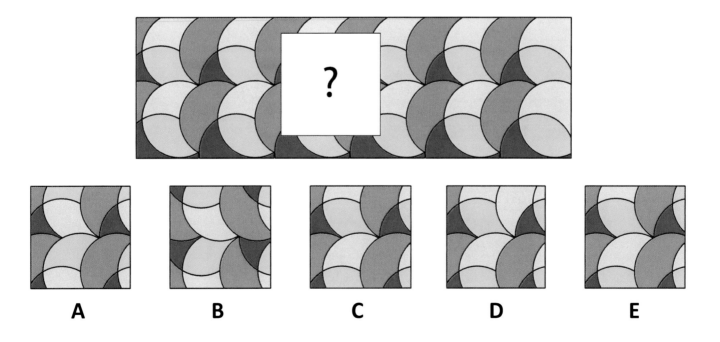

3.

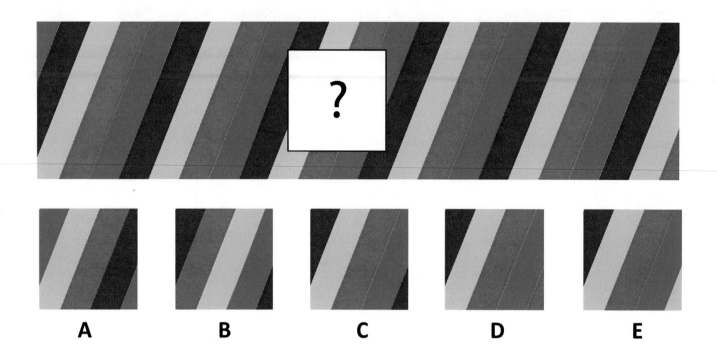

4.

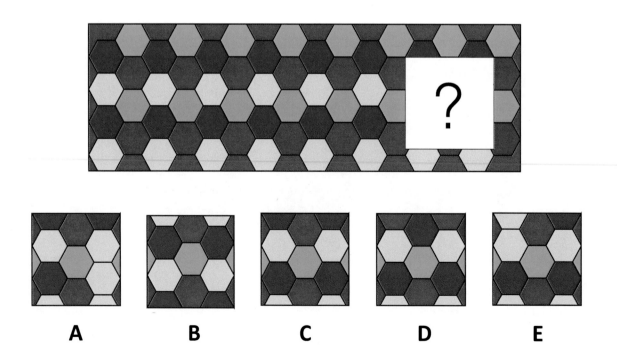

5.

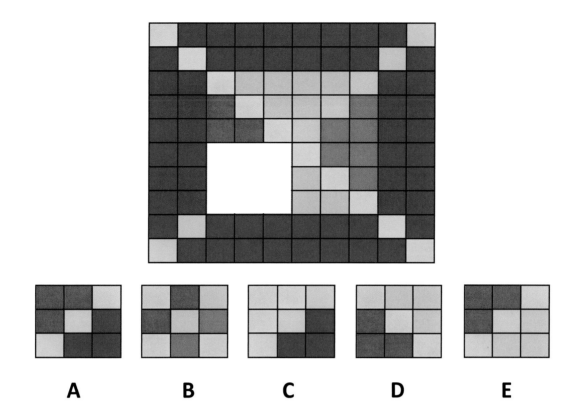

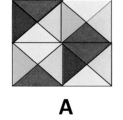 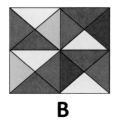 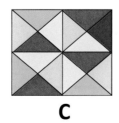 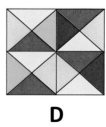 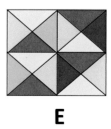

A   **B**   **C**   **D**   **E**

6.

A   **B**   **C**   **D**   **E**

7.

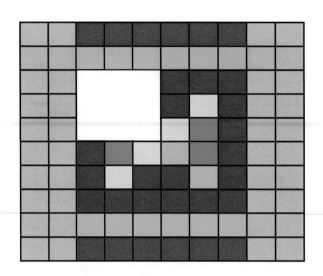

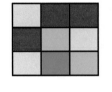  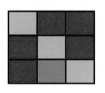 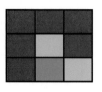

A **B** **C** **D** **E**

8.

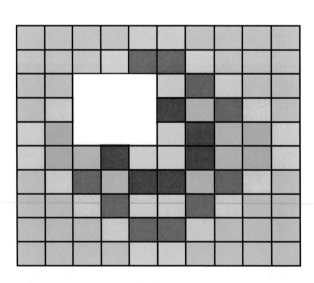

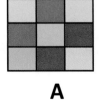 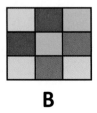 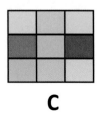 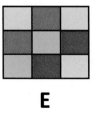

A **B** **C** **D** **E**

9.

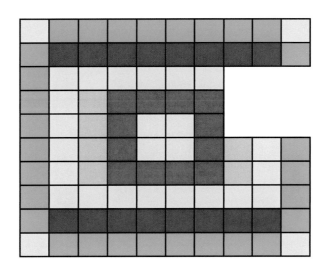

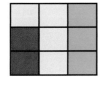 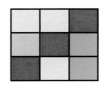 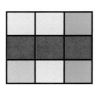 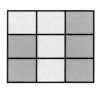

A	B	C	D	E

10.

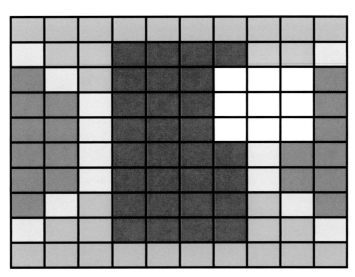

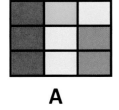 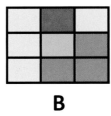 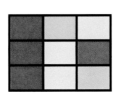 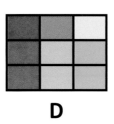 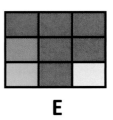

A	B	C	D	E

PRACTICE TEST 1 REASONING BY ANALOGY

Reasoning by Analogy

Students are provided with a 3X3 matrix with the image missing in one cell. They have to understand how the pictures change in the first and second rows, moving from left to right and find the missing image that has the same type of correlation with the two shapes in the lower line.

Example

CHOOSE ANSWER

1   2   3   4   5

How the pictures change in the first and second rows, moving from left to right?

In the first 2 rows, the image on the left doubles and 2 identical overlapping images result. Then, the two overlapping images move away horizontally from each other.
Following the same logic in the third row, we can understand that the correct answer is the number 5.

1

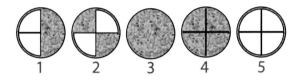

CHOOSE ANSWER

2

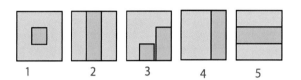

CHOOSE ANSWER

3.

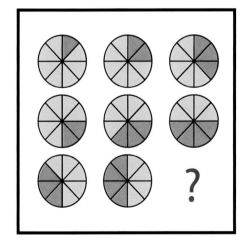

CHOOSE ANSWER

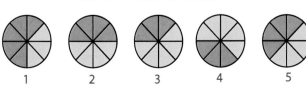

4.

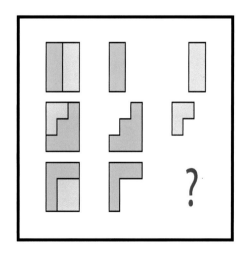

CHOOSE ANSWER

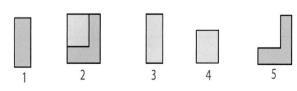

5.

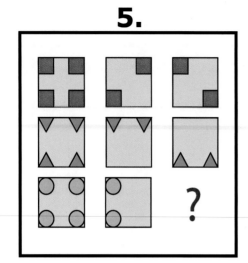

CHOOSE ANSWER

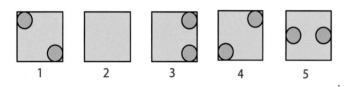

1   2   3   4   5

:

6.

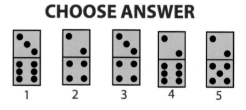

CHOOSE ANSWER

1   2   3   4   5

:

7.

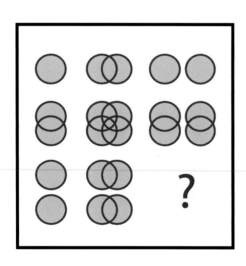

CHOOSE ANSWER

1   2   3   4   5

8.

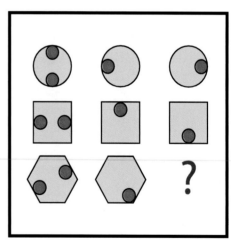

CHOOSE ANSWER

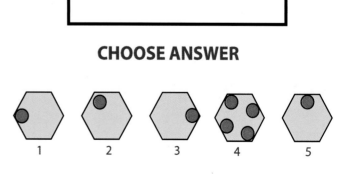

1   2   3   4   5

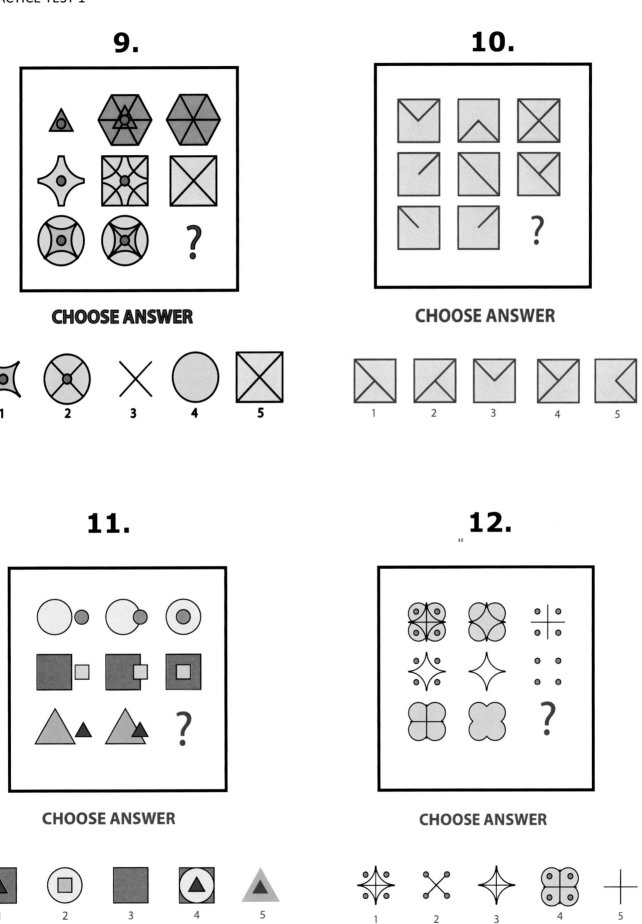

9.

CHOOSE ANSWER

1   2   3   4   5

10.

CHOOSE ANSWER

1   2   3   4   5

11.

CHOOSE ANSWER

1   2   3   4   5

12.

CHOOSE ANSWER

1   2   3   4   5

13.

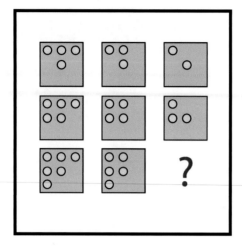

CHOOSE ANSWER

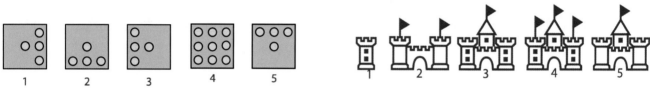

1 2 3 4 5

14.

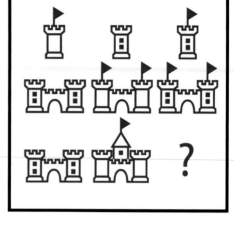

CHOOSE ANSWER

1 2 3 4 5

PRACTICE TEST 1
SERIAL
REASONING

Serial Reasoning

Students are provided with a 3X3 matrix with the image missing in one cell. They have to understand how the pictures change in each row and in each column and find the missing image that has the same type of correlation with the two shapes in the lower line and with the two shapes in the right column.

EXAMPLE

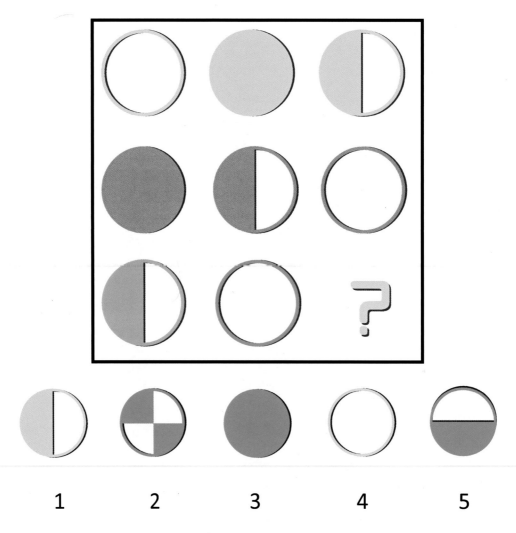

In each column, there are three different types of circles in different colors. The last column is missing a **green circle. We can exclude answers n. 1 and n. 4.**
In each row, there are three different types of circles in the same color. The lower row is missing the **full green circle.**
The correct answer is the number 3.

1.

2.

3.

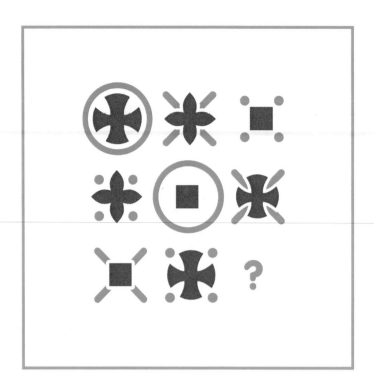

4.

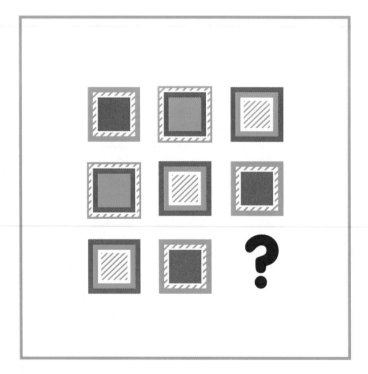

5.

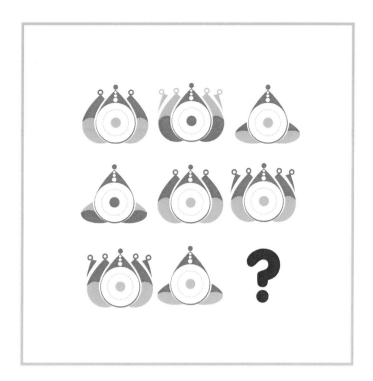

6.

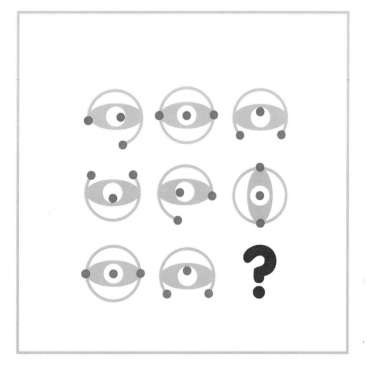

7.

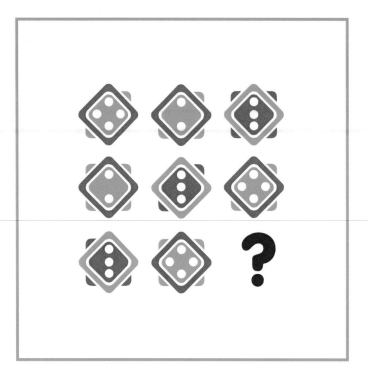

8.

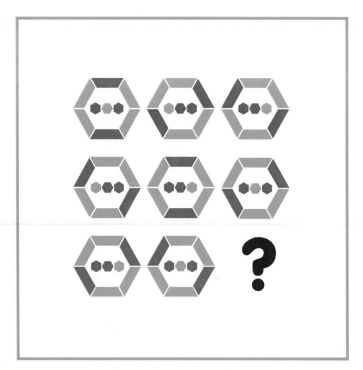

9.

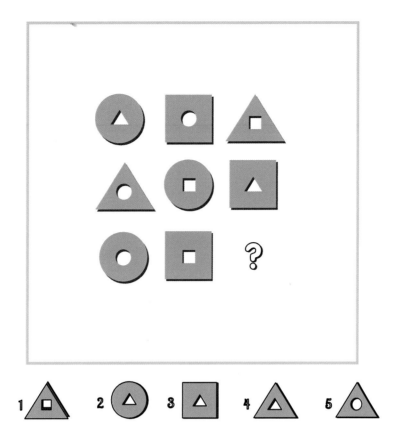

10.

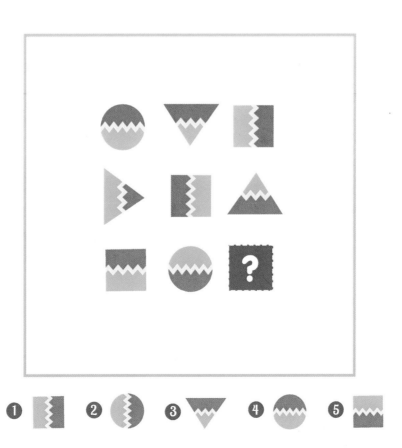

PRACTICE TEST 1
SPATIAL
VISUALISATION

Spatial Visualization - Section A

The goal of the "Spatial Visualization" section of the NNAT is to find out how two drawings will look when combined. Each question has three images on each row. The third image in each line is made by combining the first two images.

Example

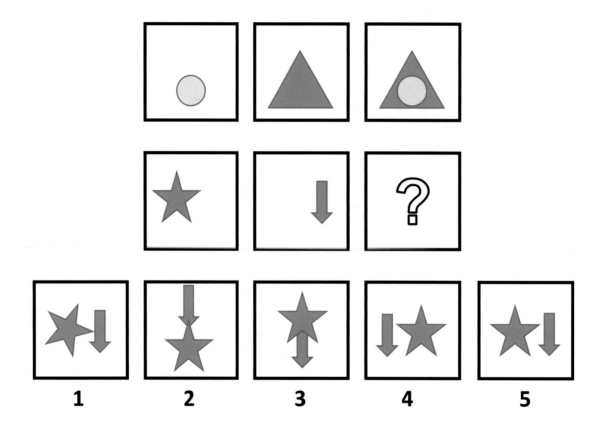

In the first row, by combining the two left pictures, we obtain a yellow circle inside a blue triangle.

In the second row, by combining the first two pictures, we obtain the image number 5, showing the same star on the left and the same arrow on the right.

1.

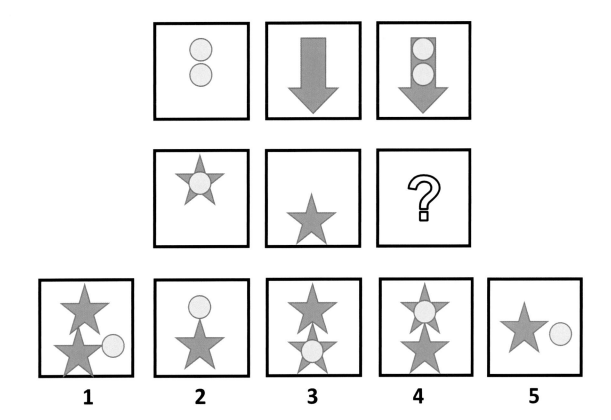

2.

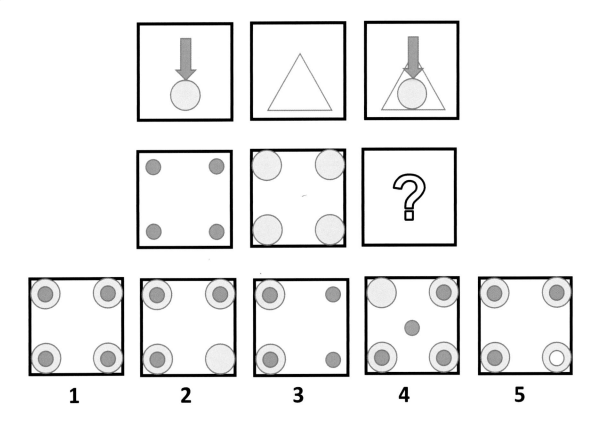

3.

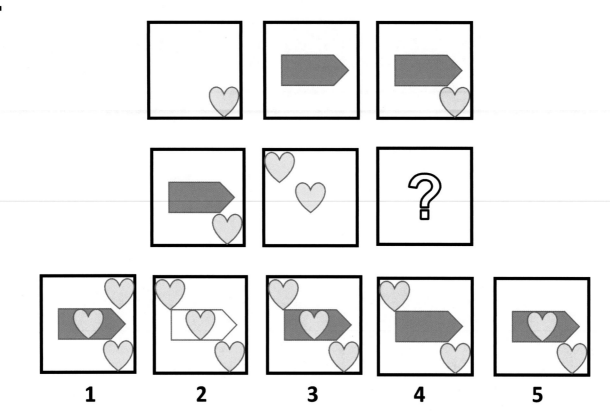

4.

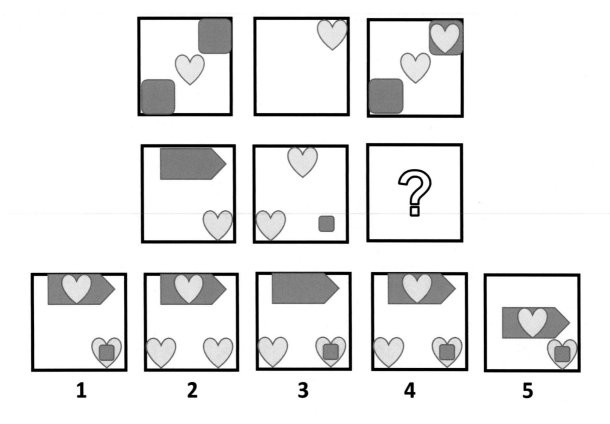

5.

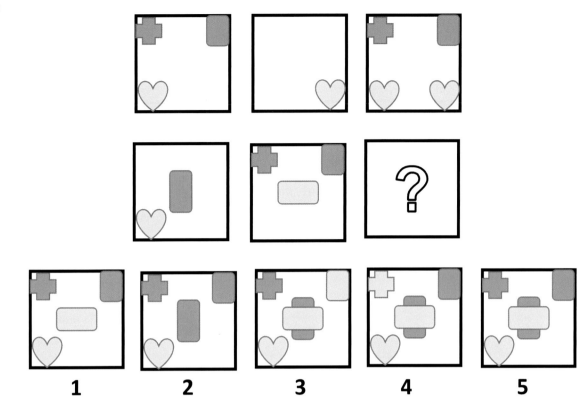

6.

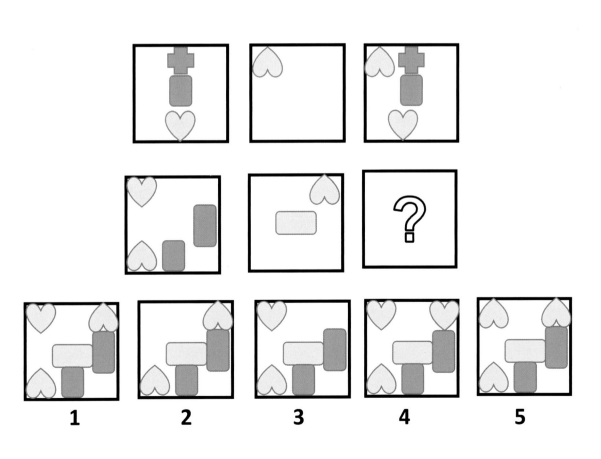

7.

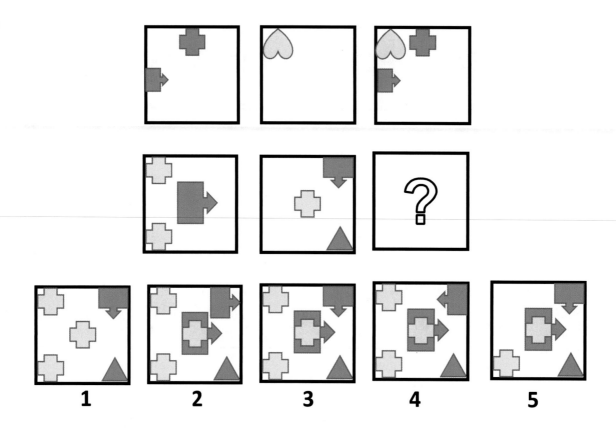

Spatial Visualization - Section B

In this section, each question has two images on each row. The second image on each row is generated by folding the outer shapes into a square.
Children must choose the answer, from the five available options, that shows what would happen if the outside pieces of the first square are folded in.
The resulting image could also be rotated, following the logic of the 2 figures in the first row.

Example

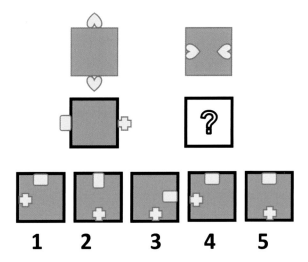

1   2   3   4   5

In the first row, the two outer hearts are folded inside the square. The resulting figure is the following:

This figure is then rotated by 90 degrees clockwise.

Following the same logic with the second row, we obtain the following figures:

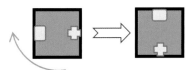

The right answer is the number 5.

8.

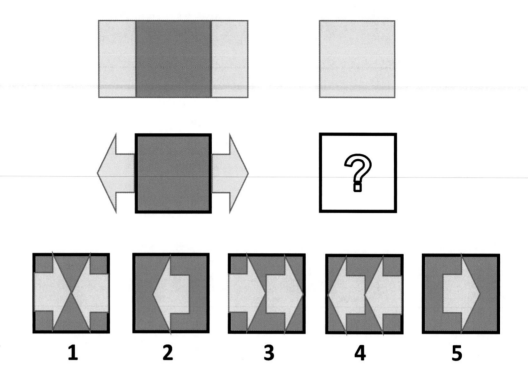

1	**2**	**3**	**4**	**5**

9

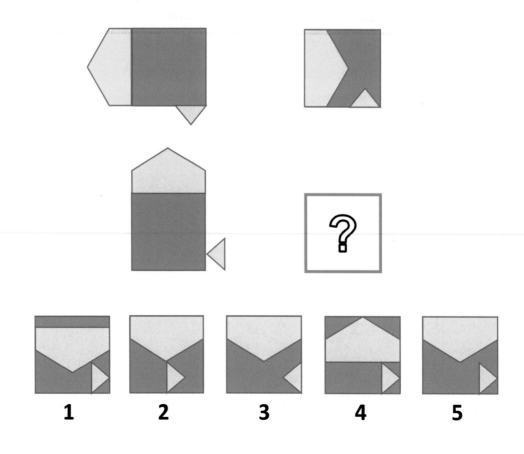

1	**2**	**3**	**4**	**5**

10.

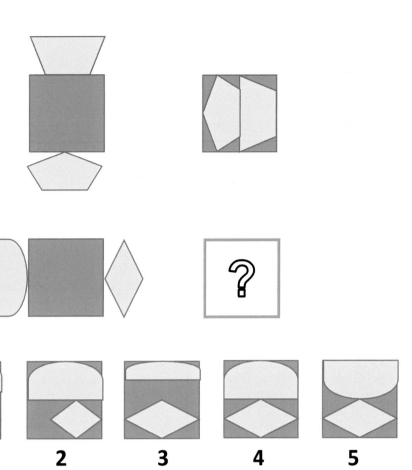

1	2	3	4	5

11.

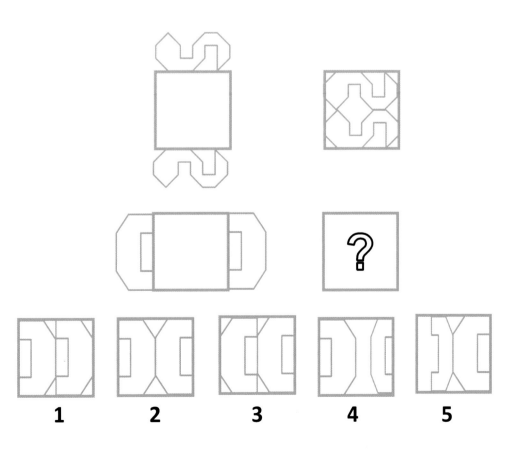

1	2	3	4	5

12.

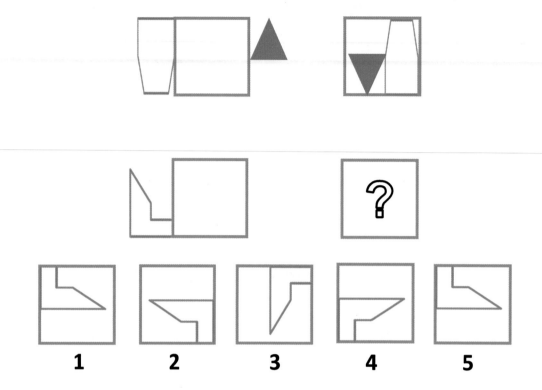

1	2	3	4	5

13.

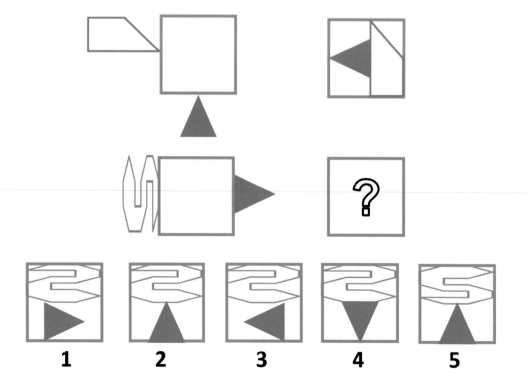

1	2	3	4	5

14.

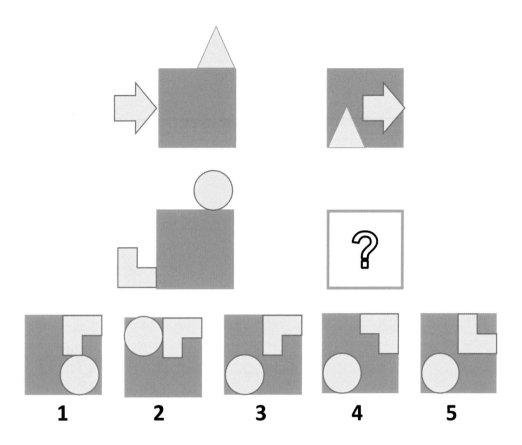

PRACTICE TEST 2
PATTERN COMPLETION

1.

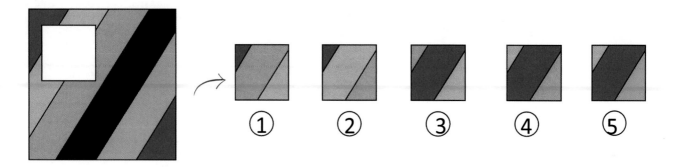

2.

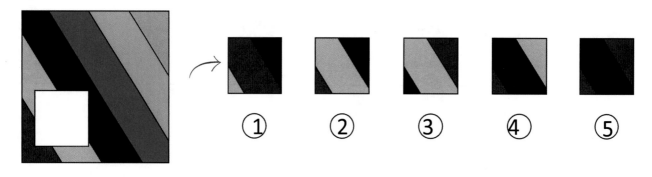

3.

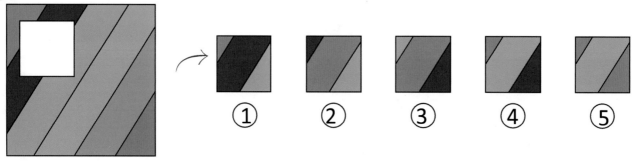

4.

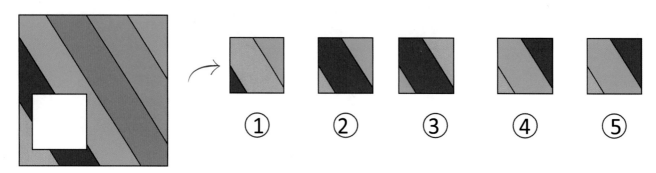

5.

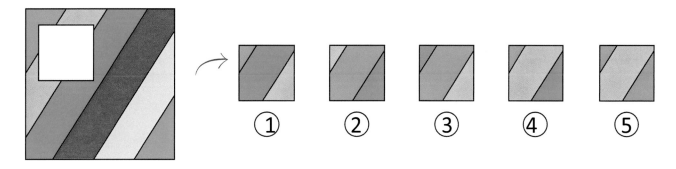

6.

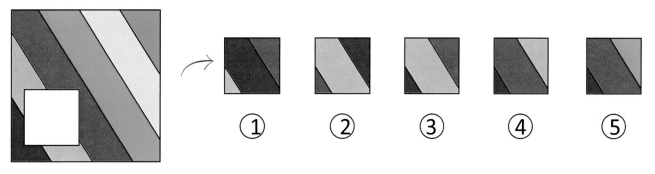

7.

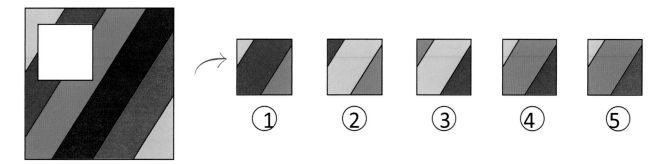

8.

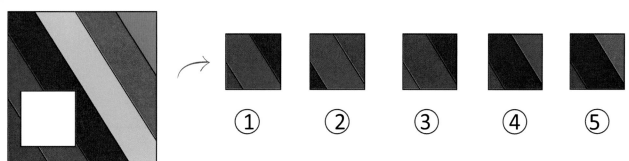

9.

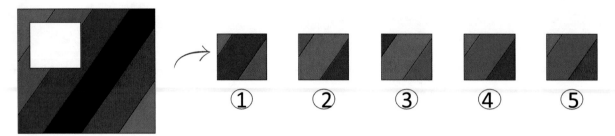

10.

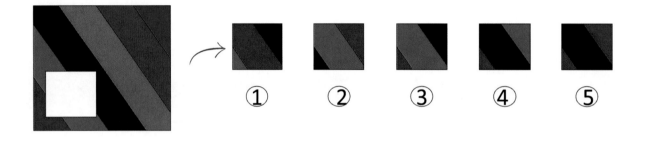

PRACTICE TEST 2 REASONING BY ANALOGY

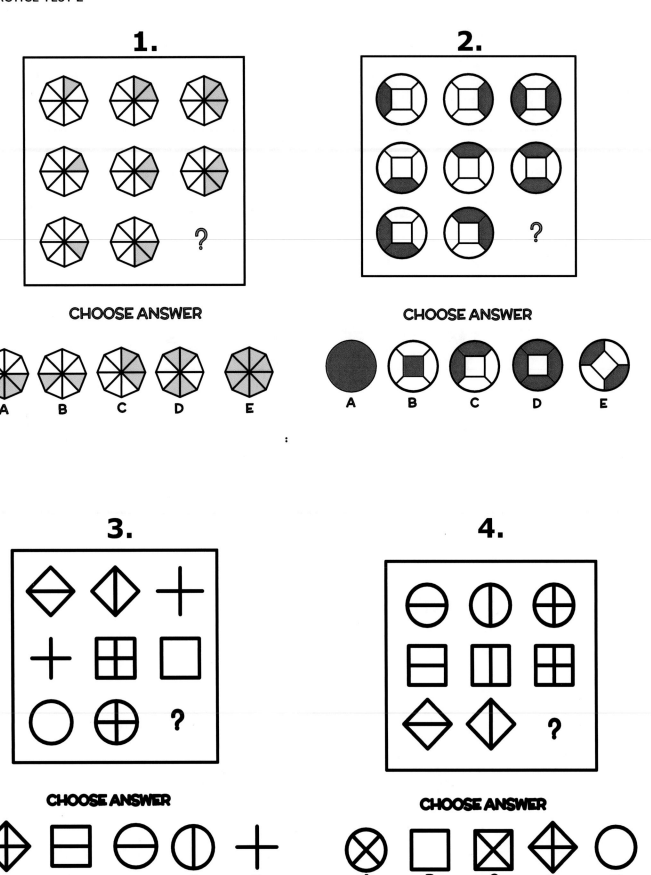

1.

CHOOSE ANSWER

A   B   C   D   E

2.

CHOOSE ANSWER

A   B   C   D   E

3.

CHOOSE ANSWER

A   B   C   D   E

4.

CHOOSE ANSWER

A   B   C   D   E

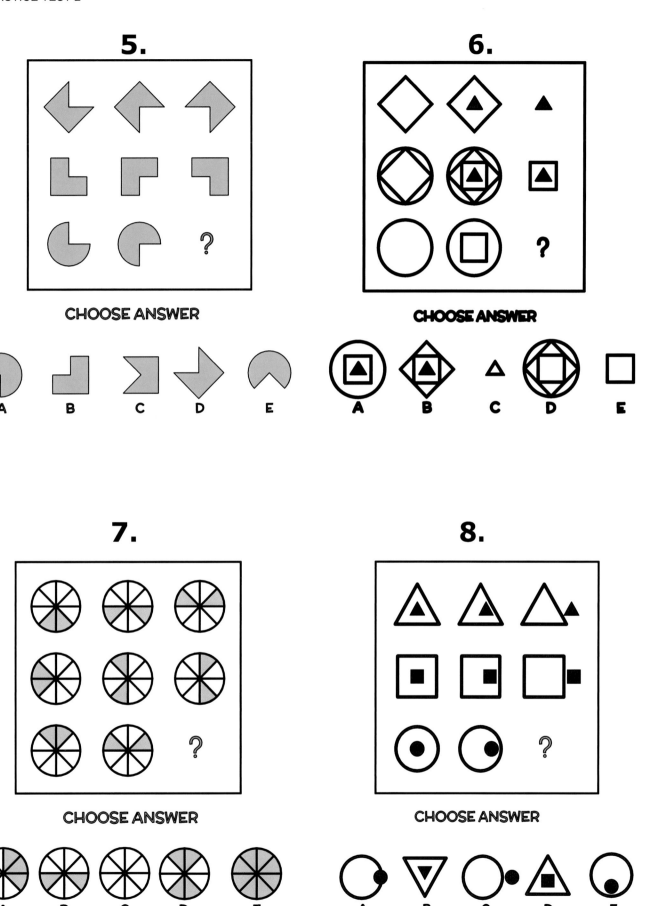

5.

CHOOSE ANSWER

A B C D E

6.

CHOOSE ANSWER

A B C D E

7.

CHOOSE ANSWER

A B C D E

8.

CHOOSE ANSWER

A B C D E

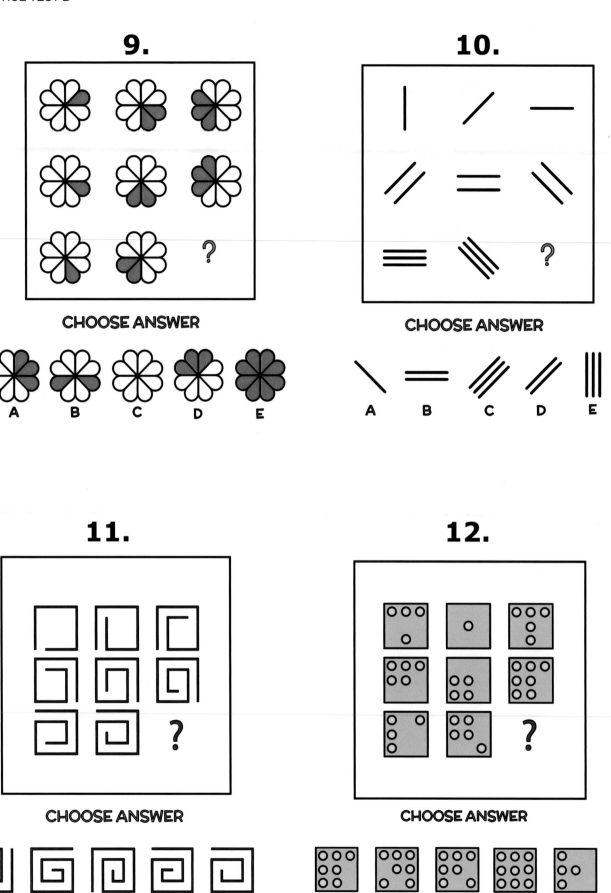

13.

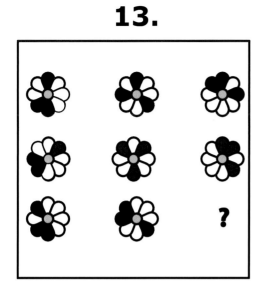

CHOOSE ANSWER

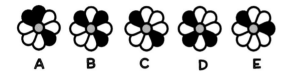

A   B   C   D   E

14.

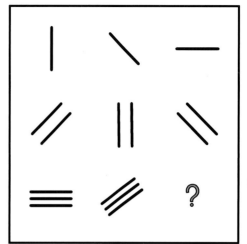

CHOOSE ANSWER

A   B   C   D   E

PRACTICE TEST 2 SERIAL REASONING

1.

2.

3.

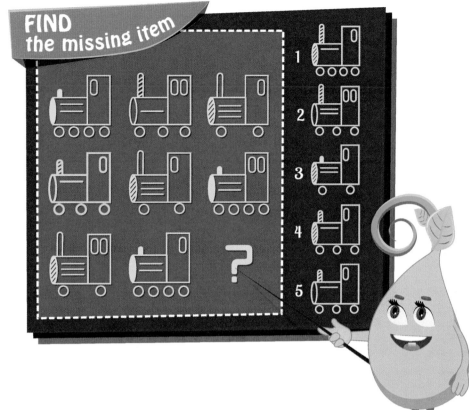

4.

5.

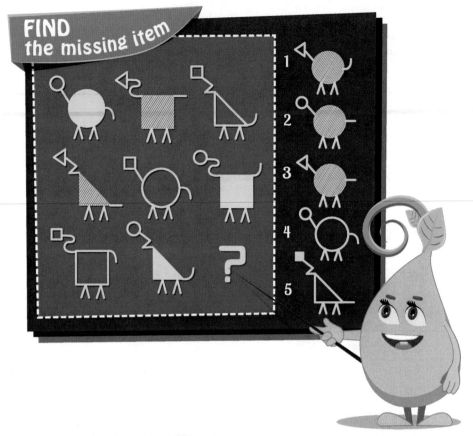

6.

7.

8.

9.

10.

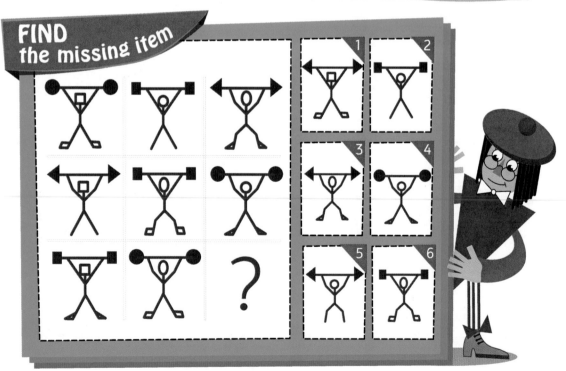

PRACTICE TEST 2 SPATIAL VISUALISATION

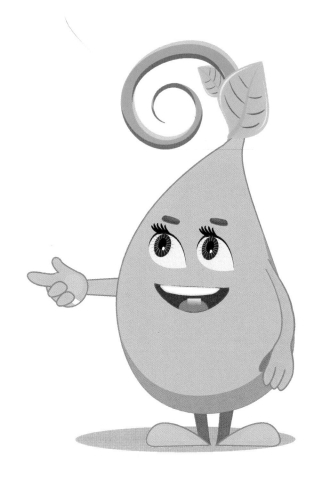

Spatial Visualization - Section A

1.

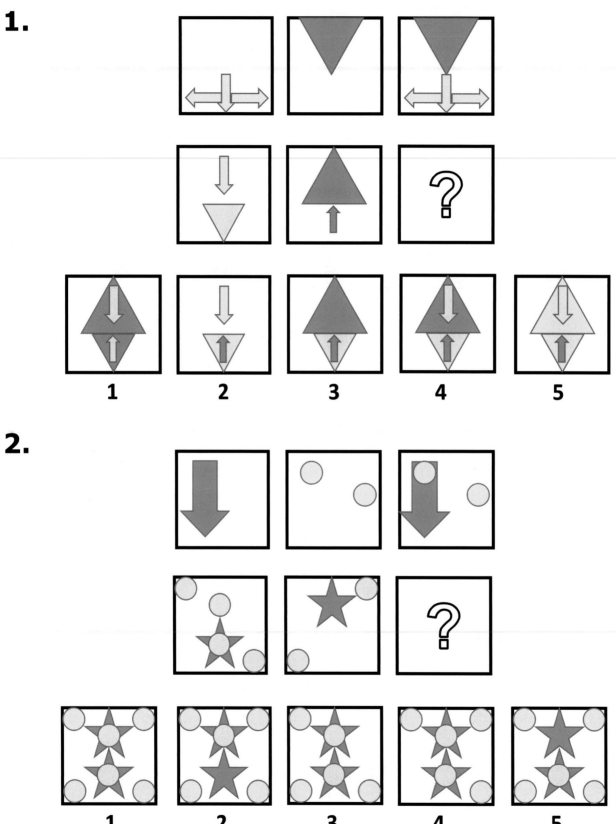

3.

4.

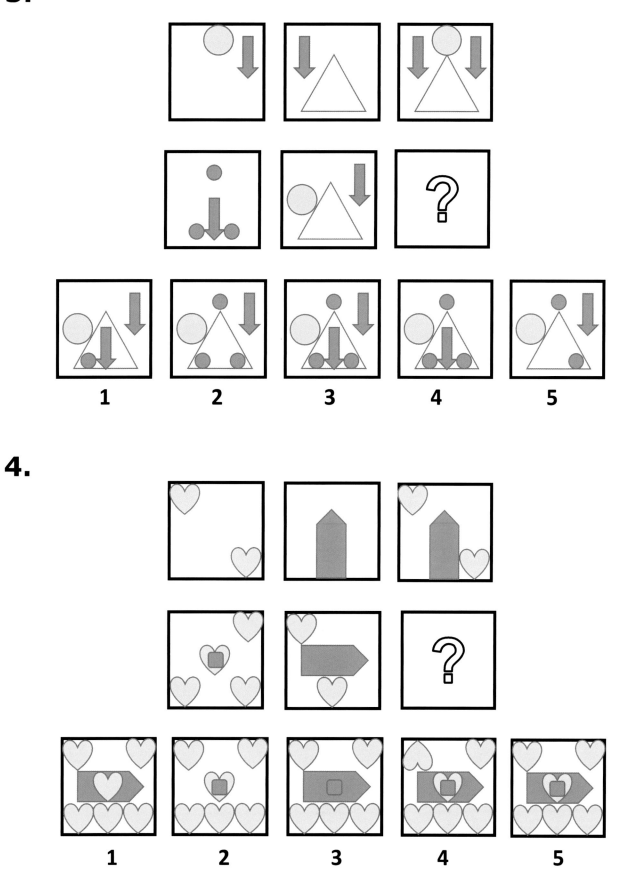

5.

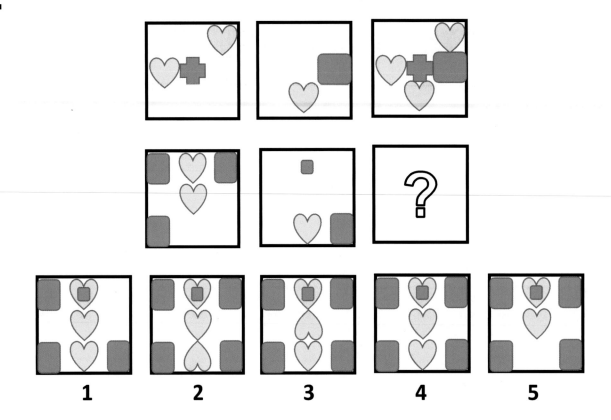

6.

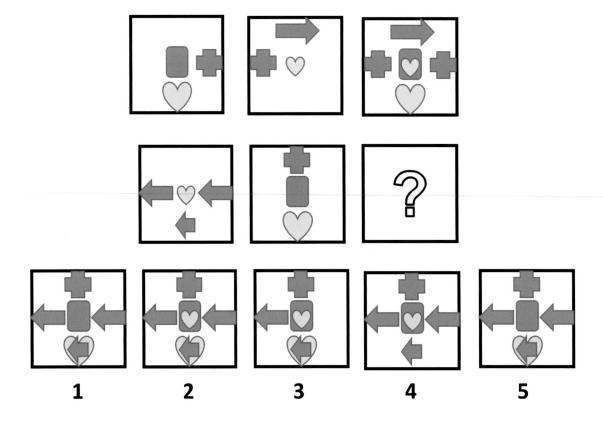

7.

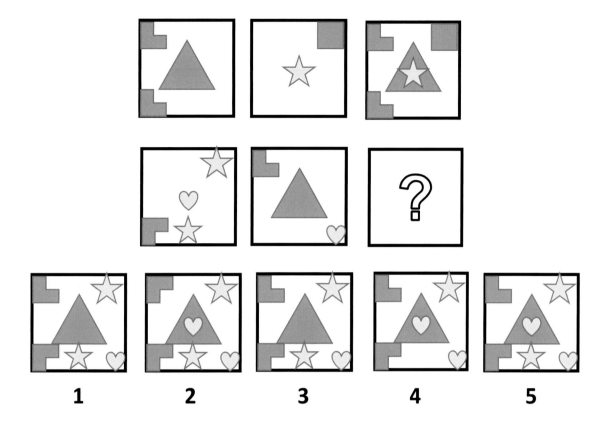

Spatial Visualization - Section B

8.

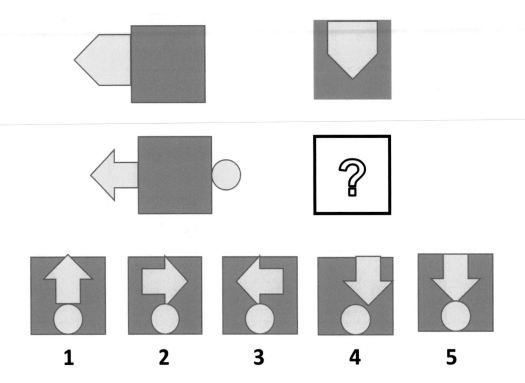

9.

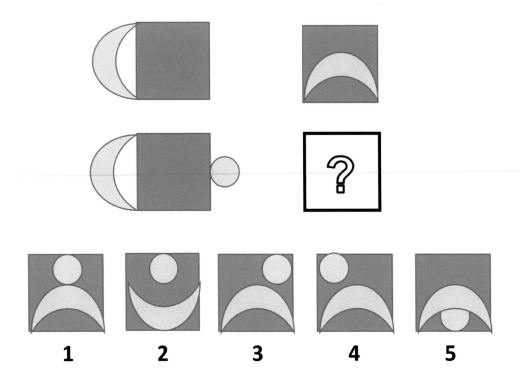

10.

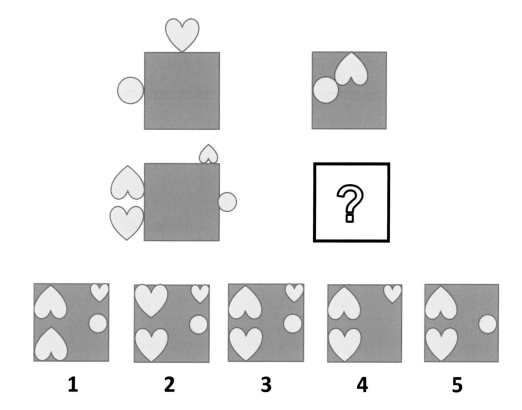

11.

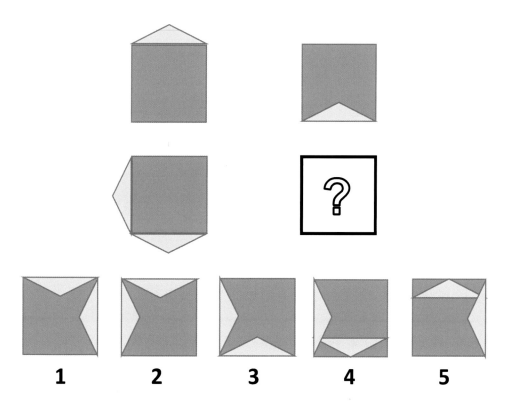

12

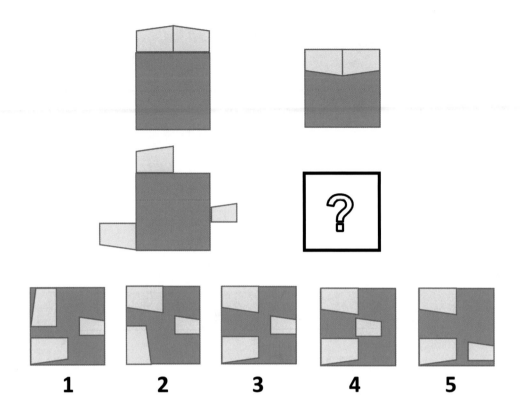

| 1 | 2 | 3 | 4 | 5 |

13.

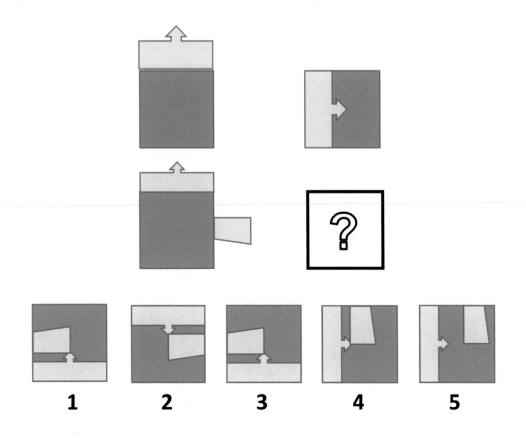

| 1 | 2 | 3 | 4 | 5 |

14.

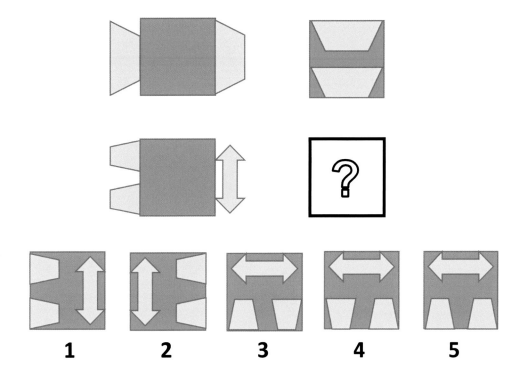

HOW TO DOWNLOAD 16 BONUS QUESTIONS

Thank you for reading this book, we hope you really enjoyed it.

PLEASE LEAVE US A REVIEW ON THE WEBSITE WHERE YOU PURCHASED THIS BOOK!

By leaving a review, you give us the opportunity to improve our work.

A GIFT FOR YOU!

FREE DOWNLOAD OF 16 BONUS QUESTIONS

Follow this link:

https://www.skilledchildren.com/free-download-nnat-test-level-d.php

You will find a PDF to download: please insert this PASSWORD: 11722

Nicole Howard and the SkilledChildren.com Team

www.skilledchildren.com

ANSWER KEY

Pattern Completion Practice Test 1
p.7

1.
Answer: option B

2
Answer: option C

3
Answer: option C

4
Answer: option C

5
Answer: option E

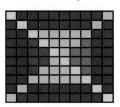

6
Answer: option E

7
Answer: option E

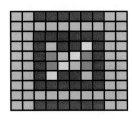

8
Answer: option E

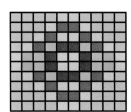

9
Answer: option B

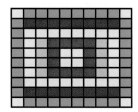

10
Answer: option A

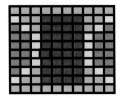

Reasoning by Analogy Practice Test 1
p.15

1. Answer: option 3. In each row, first one sector on the right is colored, then the corresponding sector on the left, and finally the combination of both sectors.

2. Answer: option 4. The inside shape grow gradually in each row from left to right.

3. Answer: option 1. The orange slices increase by one unit clockwise from left to right in each row.

4. Answer: option 4. The sequence in each row is the following: green figure and blue figure - green figure only - blue figure only.

5. Answer: option 3. The sequence in each row is the following: 4 equal elements - 2 equal elements - 2 equal elements placed in the opposite position to the previous ones.

6. Answer: option 1. The number of black dots in the upper square remains the same while in the lower square it increases by one each time.

7. Answer: option 2. The image on the left doubles and 2 identical overlapping images result. Then, the two overlapping images move away horizontally from each other.

8. Answer: option 2. The sequence in each row is the following: 2 red circles - 1 red circle - 1 red circle placed in the opposite position to the previous one.

9. Answer: option 3. A second pattern is added to the first figure (2 diagonals in the third row); then the first figure is eliminated.

10. Answer: option 3. The first and second images are combined together.

11 Answer: option 5. The outside shape gradually moves to the left, until it reaches the center of the larger figure.

12
Answer: option 5. The third image in each row is obtained by removing the second figure from the first one.

13
Answer: option 3. From each figure, proceeding from left to right, the circle at the top right is removed.

14
Answer: option 3. By superimposing the first figure on the second one, you get the third picture.

Serial Reasoning Practice Test 1
p.21

1. Answer: option 5. In each column, there are 3 different circles. Therefore, the third item in the third column could be 1, 3, or 5. In each row, the two outer dots must be at the end of the two oblique diagonals in the circle or down horizontally. The third row is missing the 2 dots placed horizontally at the bottom of the circle. Therefore, the correct answer is n. 5.

2. Answer: option 2. In each column, there are 3 different triangles. Therefore, the third item in the third column could be 2 or 4. In each row, there are 1, 2 or 3 vertical lines at the base of the triangles. The third row is missing the triangle with 1 vertical line at its base. Therefore, the correct answer is the n. 2.

3. Answer: option 2. The third column is missing the red cloverleaf. So, the answer must be n.2 or n.4. In the third row, the big blue circle is missing. So, the correct answer is n.2.

4. Answer: option 3. The third row and the third column are missing the figure with the blue square inside. Therefore, the correct answer is n.3.

5. Answer: option 2. The third column is missing the 3-pointed shape. So, the answer must be n.2, 3 or 4. The third row is missing the red dot in the circle. Let's exclude the n. 3 The 2 shapes at the bottom of the figure must be red. Therefore, the correct answer is n.2.

6. Answer: option 5. The third column and the third row are missing the following type of shape (partially open):
So, the answer must be n. 3, or 5. In each row and in each column, this type of shape has the opening oriented on the opposite side compared to the position of the red dot inside the white circle. Therefore, the correct answer is n.5.

7. Answer: option 3. Each row and column is missing the square with two dots. So, the solution must be n.3 or n.5. In each row and each column, there are 2 squares with blue background and one square with red background. So the correct answer is n.3 (blue background).

8. Answer: option 4. The third row and third column are missing hexagons with the horizontal red segments at the top and bottom.
So, the answer must be n. 2, 4, or 5. Each type of hexagon includes 3 small hexagons, 2 red and one blue. The small red hexagons can be in the following positions: side by side on the right, side by side on the left or separated from the blue hexagon. The third row and third column are missing the red hexagons placed side by side on the right. So the correct answer is n. 4.

9. Answer: option 4. The third row is missing a blue triangle. In the first column there are 2 circles, in the second column there are 2 squares, in the third column there must be 2 triangles.
So, the answer must be n. 1, 4, or 5. In each row, the larger shapes contain smaller shapes: a square, a circle, and a triangle. In the third row, the triangle contained in a larger shape is missing. So the correct answer is n. 4.

10. Answer: option 2. The third row is missing a circle. So, the answer must be n. 2, or 4. In each column, there is a circle, a triangle, and a square, but in each column, they have a different orientation compared to those in the other columns. So, we can exclude n.4 because the orientation is the same as the circle present in the first column. The solution is n. 2.

Spatial Visualization Practice Test 1
p.29

SECTION A

1. Answer: option 4
2. Answer: option 1
3. Answer: option 3
4. Answer: option 4
5. Answer: option 5
6. Answer: option 1
7. Answer: option 3

SECTION B   p.34

8. Answer: option 1

9. Answer: option 5

10. Answer: option 4 ROTATION BY 90 DEGREES CLOCKWISE.

11. Answer: option 2

12. Answer: option 3 ROTATION BY 180 DEGREES CLOCKWISE.

13. Answer: option 2 ROTATION BY 90 DEGREES CLOCKWISE.

14. Answer: option 3 ROTATION BY 180 DEGREES CLOCKWISE.

Pattern Completion Practice Test 2
p.40

1 .
Answer: option 2

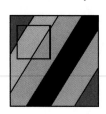

2
Answer: option 2

3
Answer: option 1

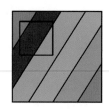

4 .
Answer: option 2

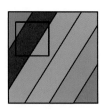

5
Answer: option 4

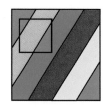

6
Answer: option 3

7 .
Answer: option 1

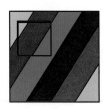

8
Answer: option 1

9
Answer: option 4

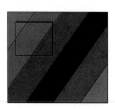

10
Answer: option 3

Reasoning by Analogy Practice Test 2
p.44

1. Answer: option A: The yellow slices increase by one unit clockwise from left to right in each row.

2. Answer: option D: The red sectors are, first, only on one side, then, also on the opposite side, and finally on both the opposite sides.

3. Answer: option E: The third picture is formed by combining the first two figures and then removing the parts found in both the first and second picture.

4. Answer: option D: The third figure is formed by combining the previous two shapes.

5. Answer: option A: The shapes rotate progressively by 90 degrees clockwise.

6. Answer: option E: The third figure is formed by what the first and second figures do not have in common.

7. Answer: option B: Proceeding from left to right, the green wedges are separated, first by 2 white wedges and then by 4 white wedges.

8. Answer: option C: The small figure inside gradually moves from left to right, until it exits the larger figure.

9. Answer: option D: In the second figure, the orange slice of the first figure rotates by 45 degrees clockwise, and a new slice is added; in the third figure, the 2 orange slices of the second figure rotate by 90 degrees clockwise, and a new slice is added.

10. Answer: option E: Proceeding from left to right, the figure rotates progressively 45 degrees clockwise.

11. Answer: option D: Proceeding from left to right, a vertical segment is added and then a horizontal segment.

12. Answer: option C: The third figure is obtained from the combination of the previous ones.

13. Answer: option E: The two adjacent petals move, one to its right and the other to its left, while the single petal remains stationary.

14. Answer: option E: Proceeding from left to right, the figure rotates progressively 45 degrees counterclockwise.

Serial Reasoning Practice Test 2
p.50

1. Answer: option 3. The third row and third column are missing the pig with 3 lines on its head. So, the answer may be n.3 or n.4. In each column, there is a single pig with partially colored legs. So, the answer cannot be the n. 4. The correct answer is n.3.

2. Answer: option 4 In each row there are 3 different shapes. Therefore, in the third row there can be circle, star or heart. Also in each column, there are 3 different shapes. So, in the third column there can be rhombus, circle or triangle. The only shape that can be in the third row and the third column at the same time is the circle. So, the correct answer can be either n.1 or n.4. Now, let's look at the small shapes at the top. In each row, there are 3 different shapes; so in the third row there can be triangle, heart or star. Also in each column, there are 3 different shapes; so in the third column there can be star, heart or rhombus. The only shapes that can be in the third row and third column at the same time might be the heart or the star. So, the correct answer is n.4, the circle with the small heart above it.

3. Answer: option 5. The third row and third column are missing the 3 wheels train. So the answer may be n.2, 4, or.5. In each row and in each column there is a train with 1 horizontal line, one with 2 horizontal lines, one with 3 horizontal lines. The third row and third column are missing the train with 1 horizontal line. We can exclude the answer n.2. In the third row and in the third column the train with a zero shifted to the left is missing. So the correct answer is n.5.

4. Answer: option 5. The third row and third column are missing the oval airplane, the rectangular wings and the single window. The correct answer is n.5.

5. Answer: option 3. The third row and third column are missing the circular shape. We can exclude the answer n.5. The third row and third column are missing the triangular head. We can exclude the answers 2 and 4. The third row and third column are missing the horizontal tail. The correct answer is n.3.

6. Answer: option 4. The third row is missing the red colored owl. So, the answer may be n.2, 4 or 5. For each color, there are 3 types of owl, Without eyebrows, with eyebrows and with closed eyes. The third column is missing the red owl with open eyes and eyebrows. The correct answer is n.4.

7. Answer: option 3. The third row and third column are missing the triangular shape. So, the answer may be n.2, 3 or 6. The third row and column are missing the dancer with her arms turned downward. The correct answer is n.3.

8. Answer: option 3. The third row is missing the cat with the squared body. So, the answer may be n.1, 3, 4 or 6. The third column is missing the cat with the triangular head. So, the answer may be n. 3, or 4. The third row is missing the cat with the tail pointing to the right. The correct answer is n.3.

9. Answer: option 4. The third row is missing the yellow cup. So, the answer may be n.1, 3, or 4. In each column, there are 2 cups having the same shape. So the correct answer is n.4 because the yellow cuo has the same shape as the blue cup.

10. Answer: option 5. The third row and the third column are missing the little man without feet. So, the answer may be n.2 or 5. The third row is also missing the triangular shaped weights. So, the answer is n.5.

Spatial Visualization Practice Test 2
p.56

SECTION A

1. Answer: option 4
2. Answer: option 1
3. Answer: option 3
4. Answer: option 5
5. Answer: option 4
6. Answer: option 2
7. Answer: option 5

SECTION B p.60

8. Answer: option 5 ROTATION BY 90 DEGREES CLOCKWISE.

9. Answer: option 1 ROTATION BY 90 DEGREES ANTICLOCKWISE.

10. Answer: option 3

11. Answer: option 1 ROTATION BY 180 DEGREES CLOCKWISE

12. Answer: option 3

13. Answer: option 4 ROTATION BY 90 DEGREES ANTICLOCKWISE.

14. Answer: option 5 ROTATION BY 90 DEGREES ANTICLOCKWISE.

Made in the USA
Coppell, TX
27 September 2024

37786870R00045